Growing Together
Marriage Enrichment for Every Culture

DR. BOB ABRAMSON

Alphabet Resources

Growing Together - Marriage Enrichment for Every Culture
Published by Alphabet Resources, Inc.
365 Stonehenge Drive
Phillipsburg, NJ 08865
1-908-213-2997
info@mentoringministry.com

Unless otherwise specified, the following applies to all Scripture quotes. Scripture taken from the New King James Version. Copyright © 1982 by Thomas Nelson, Inc. Used by permission. All rights reserved.

Scripture quotations marked (NLT) are taken from the Holy Bible, New Living Translation, copyright © 1996, 2004, 2007. Used by permission of Tyndale House Publishers, Inc., Carol Stream, Illinois 60188. All rights reserved.

Scripture quotations marked (TLBP) are taken from the Holy Bible, The Living Bible Paraphrase, copyright © 1971. Tyndale House Publishers, Inc. Carol Stream, Illinois 60188. All rights reserved.

Scripture quotations marked (NIV) are taken from the Holy Bible, New International Version®, NIV®. Copyright © 1973, 1978, 1984 by Biblica, Inc.™ Used by permission of Zondervan. All rights reserved worldwide. www.zondervan.com

Scripture quotations marked "ICB™" are taken from the International Children's Bible®. Copyright © 1986, 1988, 1999 by Thomas Nelson, Inc. Used by permission. All rights reserved.

Cover design by Ryan Stacey

10 digit ISBN 0-9843443-4-9
13 digit ISBN 978-0-9843443-4-5

Library of Congress Control Number: 2010926421

Contact Dr. Abramson by visiting
www.mentoringministry.com

CONTENTS

PART I - GROWING TOGETHER

PART II - GOD'S LOVE AND YOUR HEARTS

PART I

GROWING TOGETHER

INTRODUCTION

Consider a flower garden in early spring. When it is planted, it has great promise to produce beautiful flowers. Whether or not the garden's potential is reached depends on the care and attention given to it. As the flowers begin to grow, if they are watered and properly cared for, the result is the fulfillment of the garden's design. Together, the flowers become a thing of great beauty. If however, the garden is not properly watered and cared for, and if weeds are allowed to choke the flowers, they never flourish or grow to their full potential. When little attention is paid to nourishing the flowers, they will fade. They will be starved for the things necessary to become a beautiful garden.

Marriage can be compared to a flower garden. When the vows are first made, the marriage has great promise. It can grow into a thing of beauty, pleasing the marriage partners and the Lord. It can become a testimony to the perfection of God's design. If however, it is not properly cared for, nourished and cherished, it will never reach its potential. It will never shine for God's glory, as it might have.

1

Unlike flowers, that have no control over their own care, every couple has the ability to nurture their own marriage garden. The quality of their lives together will reflect how they care for their marriage. *"Growing Together"* provides you with information about how to nourish and enrich your marriage. It is designed to be read together by husband and wife. It will challenge both of you to take your marriage to places of richness, great joy, satisfaction and fruitfulness. It can also be of great interest to those who are contemplating marriage, or simply want to learn more about God's design for the marriage relationship.

"Growing Together" is intended to cross Christian denominational lines and work in every culture. It explores ways to enrich Christian marriage, regardless of cultural setting and context. It works equally well for single-culture and cross-cultural marriages. If you have a cross-cultural marriage, you will find *"Growing Together"* particularly valuable because its principles will transcend your two cultures. It will give you guidance on how to go about enriching your marriage God's way.

I have written *"Growing Together"* from a Christian viewpoint. The principles you will discover in the book are universal. They have their foundations in God's completely dependable Word.

(2 Timothy 3:16 NKJV) "All Scripture is given by inspiration of God, and is profitable for doctrine, for reproof, for correction, for instruction in righteousness,"

As you read the pages that follow, allow that inner voice of the Holy Spirit to help you apply what you read to your own marriage.

Chapter 1

GOD'S VIEW OF MARRIAGE

Every person enters marriage with his or her own way of doing things. We all have ideas of what is right or wrong. When two individuals' personal standards are measured against each other, it may be difficult to reconcile them. However, there is never doubt about right or wrong when we accept the guidance of the Word of God.

"Growing Together" will give you insight into ways to enrich your marriage. God wants a very real part in designing your relationship as husband and wife. He wants you to have an even better life, and will help you build on the good things you already share in your marriage experience.

For Christians, there are no better paths to travel than the ones we are given in God's Word. It is our responsibility to hear what the Holy Spirit is saying and then to follow His lead. The Bible tells us that He is our Guide and our Helper.

(John 14:26 NKJV) "But the Helper, the Holy Spirit, whom the Father will send in My name, He will teach you all things, and bring to your remembrance all things that I said to you."

(John 16:13a NKJV) "However, when He, the Spirit of truth, has come, He will guide you into all truth;"

In John 14:6, Jesus said, *"I am the way the truth and the life."* We would be wise to follow His way because it is always truth and always brings life. As you begin your time together in study, agree to be led by the Spirit of God. He will guide you into the truth that the Lord Jesus Christ has provided in His Word.

Consider the following description of how God sees marriage between a man and a woman.

GOD'S VIEW OF MARRIAGE
☑ ONE FLESH
☑ A COVENANT AGREEMENT
☑ A PARTNERSHIP

ONE FLESH IS A GOD IDEA.

(Genesis 2:24 NKJV) "Therefore a man shall leave his father and mother and be joined to his wife, and they shall become one flesh."

(Ephesians 5:31 NKJV) "For this reason a man shall leave his father and mother and be joined to his wife, and the two shall become one flesh."

In Ephesians 5:31, Paul restated what the Lord Jesus Christ said in Matthew 19 and Mark 10. Marriage is still one flesh, a covenant relationship and a partnership. It remains God's design and His will for His creation.

GOD LOOKS AT A MARRIED COUPLE AS ONE TOGETHER.

Marriage is God's way of weaving the destinies of two people onto a single path. God's Word does not say, "They shall be like one flesh," or "appear to be one flesh." It simply says, *"the two shall become one flesh."* In God's eyes, you and your spouse are one.

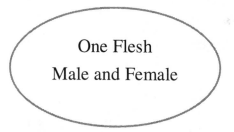

One Flesh
Male and Female

WHAT IS COVENANT?

When you are married, in God's eyes you are joined in a holy covenant. A covenant is defined as an agreement between two or more persons. In particular,

7

the marriage covenant is an agreement between husband, wife and the Lord. The Hebrew word for covenant is *b'rith.* Its root meaning is "bond" (to glue together permanently).

(Malachi 2:14b NKJV) "...Yet she is your companion And your wife by covenant."

HEAVENLY MATHEMATICS

GOD
+ HUSBAND
+ WIFE
= THE MARRIAGE COVENANT

God places the highest priority on the marriage covenant. Since a husband and wife have absolute intimacy, they must have absolute covenant. The marriage covenant is a three-fold bond of love. All three parties are to be committed to it. Remember, the third party is the Lord.

(Ecclesiastes 4:12b NKJV) "...and a threefold cord is not quickly broken."

The foundation of marriage is not romance or emotion, but a rock-solid commitment to a covenant. If we believe our commitments to Christ and to the kingdom of God are covenant commitments, we will see our obligation to the person we are married to as a direct expression of these commitments.

MARRIAGE: A PARTNERSHIP OF GRACE

1 Peter 3:7 describes a husband and wife as, *"being heirs together of the grace of life."* God's Word says that there is a partnership between them. God is not saying that they are alike, or have the same giftings or responsibilities. He is saying that they are to be in agreement, and to work together, as two who jointly inherited His favor.

> *(Genesis 2:18 NKJV) "And the LORD God said, "It is not good that man should be alone; I will make him a helper comparable to him.""*

In Genesis 2:18, God did not say, "I will make him another exactly like him." The Lord said, *"I will make him a helper, comparable to him."* God intended both husband and wife to be equal in worth, in His eyes and in the eyes of each other.

As *"heirs together,"* husband and wife have the same standing before God. There is no place in Scripture that says the wife is to be under the feet of her husband. She is not commanded to forego her own desire to be productive and fulfilled. To the contrary, she is to be like the Proverbs 31 woman. She is to be an achiever, who has made godly choices, among which are to be in submission to, and stand with her husband, as he loves her with Christ-like love.

> *(Ephesians 5:22 NKJV) "Wives, submit to your own husbands, as to the Lord."*

9

(Ephesians 5:25-26 NKJV) "Husbands, love your wives, just as Christ also loved the church and gave Himself for her, {26} that He might sanctify and cleanse her with the washing of water by the word"

Through the circumstances of life, both husband and wife are to help each other do the will of God in their marriage. They are to take this Scriptural attitude toward each other with the utmost seriousness:

(Philippians 2:3-4 NKJV) "Let nothing be done through selfish ambition or conceit, but in lowliness of mind let each esteem others better than himself."

GOD SEES HUSBAND AND WIFE AS A TEAM, WITH NEITHER BETTER THAN THE OTHER.

(Romans 2:11 NKJV) "For there is no partiality with God."

Scripture clearly teaches that God treats everyone the same. We are to follow the example of the Lord and not look down upon others. How much more should this truth be applied in our marriages? We are to see each other as God sees us. We are partners with different responsibilities and tasks, but equal in His sight. Our actions are to be a reflection of this truth. This may require a serious change in our attitudes.

However, to do less is to be in rebellion to God's Word, and His example.

In God's eyes, Christian marriage is a relationship of agreement, with both husband and wife working to insure they allow, and do not hinder, the flow of God's grace in their lives together.

YOUR MARRIAGE WILL ONLY BE SUCCESSFUL AND ENRICHING TO THE DEGREE THAT YOU ALLOW GOD'S GRACE TO FLOW THROUGH IT.

WHAT IS GOD'S GRACE AND WHY IS IT IMPORTANT?

(Ephesians 2:8-9 NKJV) "For by grace you have been saved through faith, and that not of yourselves; it is the gift of God, {9} not of works, lest anyone should boast."

Generally speaking, grace may be defined as God's unmerited favor. It cannot be earned. It is a gift. God will move sovereignly as He chooses, but most of the time, His grace flows through people. When we are willing, we become conduits or dispensers of His grace.

Grace is the goodness of God, stored up in heaven, just waiting for your willingness to allow it to flow through you to your spouse. Your willingness in action can be called real love - God's kind of love.

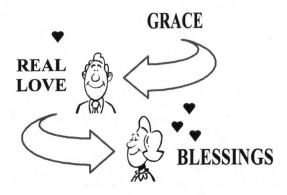

Real love is your deliberate, active, living effort to bring to your marriage partner, as much of God's grace as possible, at whatever the cost to you. Real love is seen in the flow of God's grace through you to your spouse.

Your marriage becomes better or greatly enriched, when your obedience makes room for God to work. Ask the Holy Spirit to bring His ever-increasing abundance of blessings into the midst of your marriage relationship. God's desire is to make it even finer than it ever has been. He wants to supply an abundance of His blessings in your lives. Enrichment means to supply with riches; to add greater value to a thing; to adorn or decorate; and, to make finer in quality. Pray for God to open your heart to receive these truths about marriage, for it comes out of His Word. Pray to be forever changed by it, so that your marriage can be truly enriched.

Chapter 2

HUSBAND AND WIFE: DIFFERENT BY GOD'S DELIBERATE DESIGN

UNDERSTANDING THE DIFFERENCES BETWEEN "DOING" AND "BEING"

(Genesis 2:15 NKJV) "Then the LORD God took the man and put him in the garden of Eden to tend and keep it."

God placed the first man, Adam, in the Garden of Eden and commanded him to tend it. To this day, a husband finds great satisfaction and fulfillment in tending the garden, or "doing" work. Work and its accomplishments are a driving part of his emotional makeup. This does not mean he ignores his need to "be" a companion to his wife. He simply has a God-given urgency to "do" work. He may be no more capable than his wife of doing a particular task, but he was created with a dominant felt-need to be working.

Like her husband, a wife is likely to find great satisfaction in "doing" what gives her fulfillment in a

13

career, or by excelling in a particular task. In addition, God has designed a wife's role to include a weighty need and strong gratification in "being" at her husband's side. Sharing life's moments, and feeling included in his life carries a high priority, because God created her with that special quality and gift of "being" a helpmeet or helper. (Genesis 2:18)

It is normal for husbands to see their jobs, or other acts of labor, as an expression of their caring for their wives and children. Men are built to show love by actions that may seem unrelated to the intimate expressions of love their wives want. This can lead to misunderstanding and feelings of sadness or loss by their wives. They may feel their husbands do not care about them as they should.

Bringing in a crop of vegetables, managing a store, painting the fence around the house, pastoring a church or designing a successful computer program, can be ways a man expresses his love and devotion.

Often a man finds himself spending many hours at work, or even when home, "doing" things he sees as sacrificial, necessary and fulfilling. However, his wife may feel neglected for lack of attention. Her perception of his apparent unwillingness to share great parts of his life with her can be upsetting. It can send easily misunderstood signals. His absence or distance is a potential cause of trouble. Even when he is physically present with his wife, he may be so involved in what he is "doing," that he is unaware of her legitimate wish to be acknowledged and cared for.

Both husband and wife need to understand that absence from each other, whether physical or emotional, gives the devil room to come in. Absence does not make the heart fonder. God created husband and wife to be one together, as close as a pair of praying hands.

MARRIED WOMEN VALUE THEIR HUSBAND'S UNDERSTANDING

A woman wants her husband to notice her and give her his time. She wants him to hear and care about how she feels. A woman loves the interaction with her husband, when he expresses an interest in her hopes and dreams, and the every-day challenges of her life.

In many marriages, a woman spends so much time working, that she and her husband lack time together. He may take it as a signal that she would rather be away from him. This misunderstanding may cause him to hold back his affections. He might fail to see she is emotionally in need of him expressing his love to her. As a result, she will feel she is taken for granted. She too will feel the loneliness and rejection he feels. Consequently, there will seldom (or perhaps never) be any true, meaningful closeness.

However, in the midst of their busy lives, when a husband makes the effort to keep communicating his love and understanding, his wife will know contentment and security. She will communicate the same to him. They will enjoy true closeness. They will nourish their love, as they cleave to one another.

Understanding both your basic differences *and* similar needs will help you become better marriage partners. This newfound understanding will empower your marriage to become stronger and richer. For example:

☑ Men, knowing that you may have to work at understanding your wife's feelings, will help you better communicate your love and care to her. She will be more secure, fulfilled and content. You will share an enriched marriage experience. In the midst of all your "doing," take time to "be" her companion.

☑ Women, knowing that your husband may disproportionately express his love for you through his labors, will help you understand when he seems pre-occupied with work, or does not spend as much time with you as you would like. Let him know you appreciate all he is "doing" for you.

REAL LOVE GROWS OUT OF KNOWING.
KNOWING BRINGS CARING AND UNDERSTANDING.

OUR ATTITUDES AND ACTIONS

The Book of Ephesians is a great source for guidance in overcoming things that would drive your marriage apart, and prevent you from communicating your love and care for each other.

> *(Ephesians 5:22-24 NKJV) "Wives, submit to your own husbands, as to the Lord. {23} For the husband is head of the wife, as also Christ is head of the church; and He is the Savior of the body. {24} Therefore, just as the church is subject to Christ, so let the wives be to their own husbands in everything."*

> *"Wives, submit to your own husbands,*
> *as to the Lord."*

With all the pressures on a woman to be independent today, what makes submission to her husband inviting and sensible? The next three verses in Ephesians 5 give us the answer.

> *(Ephesians 5:25-27 NKJV) "Husbands, love your wives, just as Christ also loved the church and gave Himself for her, {26} that He might sanctify and cleanse her with the washing of water by the word, {27} that He might present her to Himself a glorious church, not having spot or wrinkle or any such thing, but that she should be holy and without blemish. {28} So husbands ought to love their own wives as their own bodies; he who loves his wife loves himself {29} For no*

one ever hated his own flesh, but nourishes and cherishes it, just as the Lord does the church."

"...but nourishes and cherishes it, just as the Lord does the church."

When a husband's attitudes and sacrificial actions nourish and cherish his wife, he has modeled Christ's own love for the church. She will gladly submit to his loving care. Both will be honoring God's Word in their relationship and will benefit equally because of it. They will experience togetherness. They will be able to share in, and celebrate each other's happiness.

TO NOURISH IS TO FEED ANOTHER SO THEY WILL GROW IN HEALTH AND BECOME STRONG.

TO CHERISH IS TO VALUE TO AN EXTREME; TO HOLD DEAR; TO WATCH OVER LOVINGLY.

The biblical values and teachings of the Kingdom of God are universal. They are God's primary guide to life. The Bible is your best source of guidance for enriching your marriage. You may be assured that it will never lead you astray. As you follow the paths directed by God's Word, you will please Him, and each other. Your marriage will flourish and you will find yourselves growing ever closer to each other, and to God.

☑ Husbands, look to the cross for your example of love.

☑ Wives, look to Christ. He is your example of submission.

☑ Look for the love of God in each other.

☑ Honor Christ by submitting to each other.

(Ephesians 5:21-29 The Living Bible Paraphrase) *"Honor Christ by submitting to each other.* **You wives must submit to your husbands' leadership in the same way you submit to the Lord...**

...For a husband is in charge of his wife in the same way Christ is in charge of his body the Church. (He gave his very life to take care of it and be its Savior!) **So you wives must willingly obey your husbands in everything, just as the Church obeys Christ...**

...And you husbands, show the same kind of love to your wives as Christ showed to the Church *when he died for her, to make her holy and clean, washed by baptism and God's Word; so that he could give her to himself as a glorious Church without a single spot or wrinkle or any other blemish, being holy and without a single fault.* **That is how husbands should treat their wives, loving them as parts of themselves.** *For since a man and his wife are now one, a man is really doing himself a favor and loving himself when he loves his wife! No one hates his own body but lovingly cares for it, just as Christ cares for his body the Church, of which we are parts."*

19

SACRIFICIAL LOVE WILLINGLY GIVES ALL.
IT IS REDEMPTIVE.

MUTUAL SUBMISSION IS A CHRISTIAN CONCEPT

Mutual submission is a Christian concept. It is God's plan for a healthy and strong marriage. It requires obedience to God's will and His Word, as we show Christ-like love to one another. Mutual submission is an inward choice we make that gives outward expression of our loyalty to Christ and to our marriage partners. These outward expressions of mutual submission will never embarrass or bring shame. They will always bring blessings and rewarding enrichment to our lives.

TAKE INVENTORY: YOUR NEEDS ARE DIFFERENT BY DESIGN

We are often reluctant to tell our marriage partners what we need. As a result, these needs go unmet. Our sense of doing what we think is proper or honorable will sometimes stop us from expressing what we need. We may even feel shame when we do so. Too often, we have learned this behavior from our upbringing or circumstances. It may simply be a result of something lacking in our relationships. On other occasions, we may be afraid of how rejection will hurt us, so we do not ask our husbands or wives for what we need.

Think about what your marriage partner might need from day to day. Are there any things on the list below, that you are not yet able to give to your spouse when those times of need come?

I HAVE NOT GIVEN MY SPOUSE...

⮑ Times we can pray together	⮑	More understanding of his/her feelings
⮑ Time to be alone	⮑	The joy of receiving his/her gifts and compliments graciously
⮑ Acceptance of his/her shortcomings without anger or criticism	⮑	Commitment to him/her in some area I have held back
⮑ Some additional expression of my love	⮑	Help with raising the children
⮑ More freedom to comfortably and openly express his/her feelings to me	⮑	A less self-centered, more loving and giving attitude in our sexual relationship
⮑ More opportunity to voice his/her ideas	⮑	More time and attention
⮑ More emotional support and empathy towards him/her	⮑ Honor (This is vitally important.) ⮑ More trust

	Evidence (physical and verbal) that he/she is appreciated		What else can you identify?
			_____
			_____
			_____
			_____
			_____

Remember, God's sees your marriage as *"one flesh."* It is a covenant agreement and a partnership.

WHAT DOES EVERY MAN NEED FROM HIS WIFE?

(Genesis 2:15 NIV) "The LORD God took the man and put him in the Garden of Eden to work it and take care of it."

1. A man needs his wife to understand he is compelled by his God-given role to work. Working fulfills the following needs in a man's life. For him work is:

   ☑ a primary purpose for his life.

   ☑ a way to achieve the goals he is driven toward.

   ☑ a way for him to satisfy his role as provider for his family.

   ☑ affirmation within himself, that he has talents and abilities to do something meaningful.

GROWING TOGETHER REQUIRES A WIFE TO SEE THE VALUE HER HUSBAND PLACES ON WORKING.

A woman can help her husband maintain (and increase) his sense of worth by showing interest in what he does at work, and by encouraging him in it. She can let him know she will be content with what he provides. If a wife communicates to her husband that she trusts him to be a good provider, he will be confident in his ability to be one. He will feel secure, knowing that he is fulfilling his purpose in life. He will have a positive outlook, and be a better husband.

If you, as a wife, become critical of your husband's work, his ability to bring home money or provision; or, if you compare him to other men, you will send a signal to him that he is not up to your expectations or standards. You will be saying you are unhappy with him as your husband and provider. Be an encourager. He will love your encouragement. Your efforts will enrich your personal relationship with each other.

2. A man needs a wife with whom he can share part of himself. Ask yourself whether you, as a wife, will be a good provider of the following qualities.

☑ A FAITHFUL COMPANION
(Proverbs 31:11 The Living Bible Paraphrase) "Her husband can trust her, and she will richly satisfy his needs."

☑ AN ENJOYABLE COMPANION
(Proverbs 25:24 ICB™)" It is better to live in a corner on the roof than inside the house with a quarreling wife."

☑ A FRIEND
(Proverbs 17:17 NKJV) "A friend loves at all times, and a brother is born for adversity."

We could paraphrase this by saying,
"A wife is a friend who loves at all times..."

☑ A HELPER
(Genesis 2:18 The Living Bible Paraphrase) "And the Lord God said, "It isn't good for man to be alone; I will make a companion for him, a helper suited to his needs."

☑ A WILLING, LOVING, EXCLUSIVE SEXUAL PARTNER
(Proverbs 5:19b The Living Bible Paraphrase)
"... Let her love alone fill you with delight."

(A note to husbands: Proverbs 5:19b is not referring to selfish experience, technique or abuse. It refers exclusively to your attitudes. Your wife is your unique and wonderfully made gift from God. (Pause and reflect on this truth.) Love her as Christ loves the church. She will be your faithful and enjoyable companion, friend, helper and lover. These qualities are sure to make for a wonderful marriage partner. If you desire your wife to be all these things, be sure that you too, are a faithful and enjoyable companion, friend, helper and lover.)

GROWING TOGETHER IN MARRIAGE REQUIRES TEAMWORK.

Teamwork is a mutual effort in which husband and wife agree to work together. They purposefully and cheerfully give to each other. Although the following Scriptures refer to monetary giving, they can be applied to giving in the marriage relationship.

> *(2 Corinthians 9:6-8 NKJV) "But this I say: He who sows sparingly will also reap sparingly, and he who sows bountifully will also reap bountifully. {7} So let each one give as he purposes in his heart, not grudgingly or of necessity; for God loves a cheerful giver. {8} And God is able to make all grace abound toward you, that you, always having all sufficiency in all things, may have an abundance for every good work."*

Remember, mutual submission is a Christian concept.

It is a God idea and always results in:

☑ a better, more loving marriage.

☑ personal contentment.

☑ growing closer to each other.

WHAT DOES EVERY WIFE NEED FROM HER HUSBAND?

Carefully, look again at The Living Bible Paraphrase of Ephesians 5:25.

25

*"...And you husbands, **show the same kind of love to your wives as Christ showed to the Church** when he died for her,"*

Husbands, if you desire to become better equipped to love your wife, look to the wisdom and guidance found in seeing her as a Proverbs 31 woman. She will be deserving of the following actions on your part.

1. Lead her righteously.
   (Proverbs 31:23 NIV) "Her husband is respected at the city gate, where he takes his seat among the elders of the land."

2. Give her a secure place. She looks to you to "tend the field."

3. Give her your understanding. Listen to her heart when she speaks.

4. Give her your respect, trust and full confidence.
   (Proverbs 31:10-11 NKJV) "Who can find a virtuous wife? For her worth is far above rubies. {11} The heart of her husband safely trusts her; So he will have no lack of gain."

5. Let her know how much you appreciate her.
   (Proverbs 31:10b NKJV) "...For her worth is far above rubies."

6. Show her physically and tell her verbally how much you care for her. Make it your habit.
   (Song of Solomon 1:2 NIV) "Let him kiss me with the kisses of his mouth - for your love is more delightful than wine."

7. Honor her.

(Proverbs 31:25 NKJV) "Strength and honor are her clothing; She shall rejoice in time to come."

GIVING HER HONOR

A Christian husband has a responsibility he cannot take lightly, to think and act in ways that give honor to his wife. Dishonoring her dishonors God.

In Old Testament times, a wife was often treated as if she was more owned than honored. Unfortunately, for some men, this attitude remains to this day. God never intended a wife to be a husband's possession or property. God never designed a woman to be under a man's feet. *"Growing Together"* in marriage requires a husband to see His wife as God's special treasure for him to honor and cherish.

Honoring a wife strengthens her inner self, her true source of beauty. Having a position of honor in a marriage allows her to fulfill her calling to be a Proverbs 31 woman. Husbands, ask yourself how much honor you give your wife on a daily basis. It is easy for a man to insist on honor for himself and for his "good name." It is easy to be angry when honor among men is broken. What about God's most precious gift to you - your wife? Dishonor between marriage partners is covenant breaking. Dishonor toward your wife is disobedience to the Lord. There is ultimately a price to pay for such behavior.

COVENANT BREAKING IS DISOBEDIENCE TO GOD. IT LEADS TO DESTRUCTION. GOD'S RESPONSIBILITIES TOWARD YOU END WHEN YOUR DISOBEDIENCE TO HIS WORD BEGINS.

(Ephesians 5:1-2 NKJV) "Therefore be imitators of God as dear children. {2} And walk in love, as Christ also has loved us and given Himself for us, an offering and a sacrifice to God for a sweet-smelling aroma."

A SUCCESSFUL CHRISTIAN HUSBAND IS AN OBEDIENT COVENANT FOLLOWER OF THE LORD JESUS CHRIST.

A SUCCESSFUL HUSBAND

A successful husband is a man...
Who lives life,
laughs often,
and loves much;

Who gains the respect of intelligent men
and the love of his children;

Who knows the will of God
and lives the will of God for his life
and accomplishes his daily tasks;

Who causes his wife and children
to be blessed today,
even more than yesterday;

Who always looks for the best
and believes it of his wife, of his children,
and of the world he inhabits;

Who seeks first the kingdom of God
and His righteousness,
and gives the best that he has
to be the best he can be;

Who can say to his wife
she's the love of his life
even more today than yesterday.

A SUCCESSFUL WIFE

A successful wife...
    lives life without strife
      laughs often,
        and loves much;

    She gains honor and favor
      by her godly demeanor,
        and shows love for her husband
          with fervor;

    She knows God is with her
      His love shows forth through her,
        and His character shines from
          within her;

    She causes her husband to smile,
      and her children to grow
        in the grace and the knowledge of
          Jesus;

    She looks for the best
      and believes for the rest
        in her husband,
          her children and others;

    She seeks first God's kingdom,
      His righteousness next,
        and gives the best that she has
          to be the best she can be;

She can say to her man
he's the love of her life,
and she's grateful to God
that He made her
his wife.[1]

---

[1] Original source unknown - modified by author

Chapter 3

MARITAL LOVE: GOD'S DWELLING PLACE FOR YOU

(1 John 4:7, 9-12 NKJV) "Beloved, let us love one another, for love is of God; and everyone who loves is born of God and knows God... {9} In this the love of God was manifested toward us, that God has sent His only begotten Son into the world, that we might live through Him. {10} In this is love, not that we loved God, but that He loved us and sent His Son to be the propitiation for our sins. {11} Beloved, if God so loved us, we also ought to love one another. {12} No one has seen God at any time. If we love one another, God abides in us, and His love has been perfected in us."

Let's review our definitions of grace and love.

Grace is the goodness of God, stored up in heaven, just waiting for your willingness to allow it to flow through you to your spouse. Your willingness in action can be called real love - God's kind of love.

Real love is your deliberate, active, living effort to bring to your marriage partner, as much of God's grace as possible, at whatever the cost to you. Real love is seen in the flow of God's grace through you to your spouse.

REAL LOVE HAS A REAL PRICE.

(1 John 3:16 NKJV) "By this we know love, because He laid down His life for us. And we also ought to lay down our lives for the brethren."

If this biblical truth applies to our brothers and sisters in the Lord, how much more should it apply concerning the person to whom we are married. A successful marriage will cost both of you. Everything of value has its price. The higher the value, the higher the price. Mature marital love toward each other says:

You are worth a very high price to me. I willingly pay it because you are my treasure. I will make the effort to bring God's grace into your life, and to nourish and cherish you with His kind of love. Whatever it costs is nothing compared to how precious you are to me.

The Bible tells us that marital love rejoices with the truth (1 Corinthians 13:6). It is easy to see why. The truth the Word teaches us about love's qualities is cause for celebration. It liberates us and gives us the gift of joyful fulfillment that nothing else can.

SEVEN BIBLICAL PILLARS OF LOVE

FOR GROWING TOGETHER IN

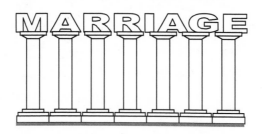

(1 Corinthians 13:4-7 NIV) *"***Love is patient, love is kind.*** It does not envy, it does not boast, it is not proud. {5} It is not rude, it is not self-seeking, it is not easily angered, it keeps no record of wrongs. {6} Love does not delight in evil but **rejoices with the truth**. {7} **It always protects, always trusts, always hopes, always perseveres.***"

1. LOVE IS PATIENT.
2. LOVE IS KIND.
3. LOVE REJOICES WITH THE TRUTH.
4. LOVE ALWAYS PROTECTS.
5. LOVE ALWAYS TRUSTS.
6. LOVE ALWAYS HOPES.
7. LOVE ALWAYS PERSEVERES.

These seven biblical pillars of love are the wisdom upon which we build our marriages. They are the supports that will not fail us when the winds and rains of life come. These pillars rest upon the Rock, Christ Jesus, who is the eternal, living Word of God. They are as sure and dependable as He is.

(1 Corinthians 13:7 The Living Bible Paraphrase) "If you love someone, you will be loyal to him no matter what the cost. You will always believe in him, always expect the best of him, and always stand your ground in defending him."

FIRST PILLAR - WILL YOUR LOVE BE PATIENT?

If you were to examine the original Greek text of 1 Corinthians 13:4 you would find it really says, *"Love suffers, suffers."* There is a word picture given here of repeated acts of patience.

The idea behind the words of the Greek text is that love is patiently, habitually exercised with a passion or determination. This kind of patience is a profoundly positive exercise and experience. It speaks of a God-given capacity for self-control, despite the circumstances. Marriage ought to be a consistent exercise of loving patience under every trial or test. The degree of patience you show will determine the degree of richness in your relationship.

(Colossians 1:10-11 NKJV) "that you may walk worthy of the Lord, fully pleasing Him, being fruitful in every good work and increasing in the knowledge of God; {11} strengthened with all might, according to His glorious power, for all patience and longsuffering with joy;"

36

(Colossians 1:11b NIV) "...so that you may have great endurance and patience..."

☑ Patience is the first pillar.

SECOND PILLAR - WILL YOUR LOVE BE KIND?

To be kind is to be considerate, compassionate, good-hearted, supportive, sympathetic, warm and tender.

When you are kind to your marriage partner, you give unselfishly to bless him or her. You become imitators of Christ, who gave unselfishly of Himself. Your marriage becomes the place where His grace will flow. Rich marital experience comes when the flow of heavenly grace is unhindered.

(Ephesians 4:32 NKJV) "And be kind to one another, tenderhearted, forgiving one another, just as God in Christ forgave you."

☑ Kindness is the second pillar.

THIRD PILLAR - WILL YOUR LOVE REJOICE WITH THE TRUTH?

Rejoicing with the truth means rejoicing in God's Word, and in your understanding of how He works in your marriage. It means putting God in the middle of your marital joy and giving no place for the devil's lies to disrupt or destroy that joy. It means being planted in a covenant garden of truth, so you may grow together to perfection. *"Growing Together"* brings enrichment and fullness to marriage.

Rejoicing over God's truth about your spouse and your marriage brings more of the goodness of God's grace to both of you. The truth is, a loving, caring attitude in marriage brings rejoicing over your spouse, who is your treasure, given to you by God.

    ☑ Rejoicing with God's truth concerning your spouse is the third pillar.

FOURTH PILLAR - WILL YOUR LOVE ALWAYS PROTECT?

The biblical word originally used in 1 Corinthians 13:7 for *"protect"* implied the idea of a covering or an element of security. Love will support, cover, protect and secure your marriage.

Each of you is to cover your spouse with loving protection, especially in those times when one of you becomes vulnerable due to a failure or shortcoming. There is a direct relationship between your ability to protect each other and your willingness to cover and secure your spouse.

    ☑ Loving protection is the fourth pillar.

FIFTH PILLAR - WILL YOUR LOVE ALWAYS TRUST?

Trusting happens when you believe every good thing about the one you love, regardless of apparent circumstances. The decision to believe the best in each other, as an act of love, will be constantly strengthened and supported by your trust in God.

When you see Christ and His Word abiding in your husband or wife, it is easy to trust, and be persuaded of all the good within them. It is very difficult to think poorly of someone whose life's testimony consistently shows the abiding presence of Christ.

In order to strengthen your trust, make every effort to let Christ abide richly within the covenant of your marriage. Make it a team effort. Do it together. This will be a powerful key to unlocking great things. Start by re-examining your present lifestyles. Look carefully at who and what you now allow to dwell in your hearts. Search out those things that might cause mistrust and become a wedge between the two of you. Bring them into the open and let love destroy them.

"Growing Together" requires trust between husband and wife. Trust is a series of decisions, which become a pattern for your thinking. It is not a reaction to the moment at hand.

☑ Trust is the fifth pillar.

SIXTH PILLAR - WILL YOUR LOVE ALWAYS BE HOPEFUL OF ALL GOOD THINGS?

Always see your marriage through positive, optimistic eyes. Hope in each other goes hand in hand with hope in God.

> *(Psalms 43:5 NKJV) "Why are you cast down, O my soul? And why are you disquieted within me? Hope in God; For I shall yet praise Him, The help of my countenance and my God."*

If hope lives in your hearts, it will live in your marriage. Loving hope between husband and wife is not a reaction to the moment at hand. It is a series of expectations, expressed in your life's decisions. Act to encourage each other to grow healthier and stronger in Christ, and with one another. *"Growing Together"* requires that, through Christ, you believe the best in each other and expect it to come to pass.

> *(Hebrews 11:1 NKJV) "Now faith is the substance of things hoped for, the evidence of things not seen."*

☑ Hope is the sixth pillar.

SEVENTH PILLAR - WILL YOUR LOVE ALWAYS PERSEVERE?

The idea of persevering love is closely tied to your ability to be patient and protective. Perseverance is work. It is a choice to keep trying, as you hold tightly to your marriage covenant. If you persevere together, in spite of what may happen, your love will continually draw its power from the abiding presence of Christ. It will stand in unchanging resolve. Nothing will be able to shake it loose from the two of you.

> *(Galatians 6:9 NKJV) "And let us not grow weary while doing good, for in due season we shall reap if we do not lose heart."*

Perseverance will come from the inner strength God provides. It will fuel the fires of hopeful expectation for a continuing good life together. It will bring the testimony that you are *"Growing Together."*

☑ Perseverance is the seventh pillar.

 Love is patient. Love is kind. Love rejoices with the truth. Love always protects. Love always trusts. Love always hopes. Love always perseveres.

These seven pillars, working together, will give you every opportunity to dwell in a loving, enriched, fruitful and satisfying marriage.

Chapter 4

COMMUNICATION: SPEAKING THE TRUTH
IN LOVE

(The Language of Biblical Closeness)

*(Ephesians 4:15 NKJV) "...**speaking the truth in love**, may grow up in all things into Him who is the head; Christ;"*

The key ingredient to understanding each other is to communicate lovingly and truthfully. Learning to speak the truth in love more willingly and more often will enrich your relationship as husband and wife.

WHAT IS SPEAKING THE TRUTH IN LOVE?

Speaking the truth in love means communicating with an unselfish, charitable, affectionate and benevolent kind of love. Look closer at what happens when you speak the truth in love.

☑ You never manipulate, deceive or try to hide evil, self-serving thoughts underneath your words.

☑ You speak with intentional transparency. As you do, you bring clarity and understanding.

☑ Your words release God's grace.

☑ What you say is rich with life. It affirms and encourages your spouse.

☑ Your words do not corrupt. There is no evil in them. They are tender, forgiving words. They could be labeled "God words," because they agree with what the Holy Spirit would say. When you speak such words to each other, you bring grace and love, and it takes you both a little bit closer to God.

Reflect on the speech patterns you typically use to communicate with your spouse. Do your words consistently carry the character of God? Do they spill His love out onto your spouse? What effect do your words typically have on you? Do they uplift and motivate you? How willing are you to make adjustments and change the character of your words so they are habitually full of life?

WHAT STOPS YOU FROM SPEAKING THE TRUTH IN LOVE?

We all have attitudes that close our hearts to God, to the guidance of His Word, and to each other. Attitudes that have been with us for a long time can be difficult to change, because we have become comfortable in them. Some even seem beyond our ability to change.

Consequently, we accept these attitudes as the way things have to be. This does not have to be the case. You can make a choice to speak the truth in love. Your words can change your attitudes. Your attitudes can change your words.

WHAT YOU SAY CAN CHANGE HOW YOU THINK.
HOW YOU THINK CAN CHANGE WHAT YOU SAY.

(Luke 6:45 NKJV) "A good man out of the good treasure of his heart brings forth good; and an evil man out of the evil treasure of his heart brings forth evil. For out of the abundance of the heart his mouth speaks."

WHAT HELPS YOU SPEAK THE TRUTH IN LOVE?

*(Ephesians 4:20-23 NKJV) "But you have not so learned Christ, {21} if indeed you have heard Him and have been taught by Him, as the truth is in Jesus: {22} that you put off, concerning your former conduct, the old man which grows corrupt according to the deceitful lusts, {23} **and be renewed in the spirit of your mind**,"*

Renewing means tearing down and rebuilding. Old structures must be demolished before new ones can be built in their place. When it comes to the patterns of our thinking, this is often a difficult thing to do.

45

However, with perseverance and a willingness to change, you can do it. A willingness to change in the spirit of our minds (our attitudes) is vital to a healthy relationship.

> *(Ephesians 4:23 NLT) "Instead, there must be **a** **spiritual renewal** of your thoughts and attitudes."*

Whatever spirit we permit to work in our minds will determine how we understand what we see and hear. Our reactions, what we say and do, follow the leading of whatever spirit has influence over our thinking. Demolish and clear away any spirit that is not of God. Remember, your attitudes will change your words.

PRACTICAL STEPS TO TRUTHFUL AND LOVING COMMUNICATION

> *(Ephesians 4:1-3 NKJV) "I, therefore, the prisoner of the Lord, beseech you to walk worthy of the calling with which you were called, {2} with all lowliness and gentleness, with longsuffering, bearing with one another in love, {3} **endeavoring to keep the unity of the Spirit in the bond of peace."***

FIRST STEP

Bring the unity of the Spirit and the bond of peace into your speech and therefore into your relationship. Here is how.

46

☑ Avoid lies, big or small. Avoid the temptation to speak half-truths. (These seemingly harmless falsehoods are lies.) Be aware that your words can become smoke screens that seem truthful, but actually veil or hide the truth. Lying in any form reveals the hardened condition of the heart. It gives place to the devil to do his destructive work in your relationship. All forms of lying have a negative impact and unintended consequences.

(Ephesians 4:24-25 NKJV) "and that you put on the new man which was created according to God, in true righteousness and holiness. {25} Therefore, putting away lying, Let each one of you speak truth with his neighbor, for we are members of one another."

☑ Do not let your anger go unresolved. It will turn into bitterness.

The Bible warns about allowing a root of bitterness to take hold. Anger and hurt feelings give the devil an opening between you and your spouse, causing division and strife. This will drive you from togetherness into isolation. In your isolation, your bitterness will deepen.

(Ephesians 4:26-27 NKJV) "Be angry, and do not sin": do not let the sun go down on your wrath, {27} nor give place to the devil."

SECOND STEP

Learn to give gifts to your marriage partner.

- ☑ Give a gift that expresses your love. It could be a flower, a note or something you do, or choose not to do. Allow truth spoken in love to accompany it.

- ☑ Give the gift of service. Anything you do that unexpectedly relieves your spouse of some burden will bring God's grace. Even without saying anything, it will communicate volumes of truth in love.

- ☑ Give the gift of your presence. Determine to spend time with each other. Take a hard look at your priorities. Give time to the marriage relationship. It will be an investment with great returns. The gift of your presence is a purely unselfish expression of love. It says, *I am taking time to pay attention to you and consider you more valuable than the things that could take me away from you.* It is the best context within which, together, you can practice and refine your communication skills.

- ☑ Among the greatest gifts you can give your marriage partner are your spoken prayers. The truths you speak in love on behalf of them have great power in the ears of your heavenly Father. They set the hand of God in motion. As your spouse hears them, they set his or her heart in motion, too.

THIRD STEP

Learn to listen. Being in a meaningful relationship requires listening to each other. Being close to your spouse is more than just proximity or physical closeness. It requires a deliberate effort to discern what his/her words mean; and, to understand the heart and spirit underneath the words. There is a close connection between spiritually listening and giving the gift of your presence.

Hanging out in the garden and occasionally sharing a piece of fruit will not do it. If Adam had listened to Eve with spiritually discerning ears, he would have left no room for sin to snake its way between them. He would have discerned the evil one behind her words and could have helped her overcome the temptation. Instead, the temptation overcame them. Listening requires a spiritual effort. We do not naturally listen with our spiritual ears. If we make the effort to listen and spiritually discern what we are hearing, it brings wisdom and reveals truth.

*(Romans 8:5-6 NKJV) "For those who live according to the flesh set their minds on the things of the flesh, but those who live according to the Spirit, the things of the Spirit. {6} For to be carnally minded is death, but **to be spiritually minded is life and peace**."*

Communicating with your spouse involves a combination of words, facial gestures and body language. These all contribute to the messages you send to and receive from each other. As you have seen, listening really involves much more than just the input gained from your five senses. It is normal in every day life to communicate carnally (with our five senses) because of our fallen, sinful state. You rely on the information your natural senses bring you. You hear words, or sense by some gesture or expression, what your marriage partner is saying. You receive the message and digest the words for what they mean to you, but what you digest may not be what your spouse intended. You may have distorted it. If you misinterpret the words, the true meaning of the message will be lost. Carnal listening has great limitations, and is filled with potential consequences and dangers.

CARNAL LISTENING

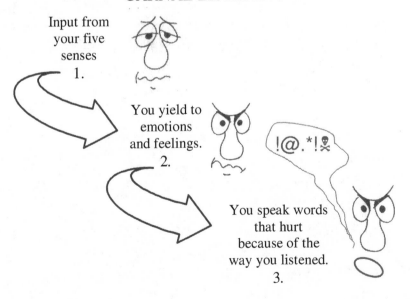

Input from your five senses
1.

You yield to emotions and feelings.
2.

!@.*!☠

You speak words that hurt because of the way you listened.
3.

1. YOU HEAR YOUR SPOUSE, AND AT THE SAME TIME, RECEIVE INPUT FROM YOUR OTHER SENSES. THE WORDS AND WHAT YOU SENSE IMPACT YOUR FEELINGS AND EMOTIONS.

2. YOUR FEELINGS AND EMOTIONS BEGIN TO CONTROL YOUR THINKING.

3. THIS RESULTS IN CARNAL, IMPULSIVE OR IMPROPER REACTIONS TO WHAT YOU HAVE HEARD.

WHAT IS WRONG WITH THIS SEQUENCE?

As you can see, carnal listening results in carnal thinking. When this happens, you fail to measure what you have heard by Christian values and standards. Instead, you allow the world's way of thinking to guide you. Consequently, how you react in response to what you have heard has potential for damaging your relationship. Your words may be harsh, uncaring or simply unwise. You have provided no room for words of grace, love, kindness and consideration. The inevitable result of carnal listening will be carnal communication.

Carnal listening allows no room for God, but forces you to operate from the place of your emotions. There is nowhere in the sequence to stop and seek guidance from the Holy Spirit. Misunderstanding and impulsive reaction then causes division and strife. Things begin to spiral out of control. Since you no longer exercise control over your feelings or actions, peace is replaced by strife. The basis for your relationship is eroded. In some measure, your covenant marriage partnership will be weakened and you grow apart from each other.

Compare the listening steps in the next diagram with the previous one. This one contains one of the keys to listening that will change the effectiveness of how you respond to each other.

LISTENING AFTER THE SPIRIT
(THE RIGHT WAY TO LISTEN)

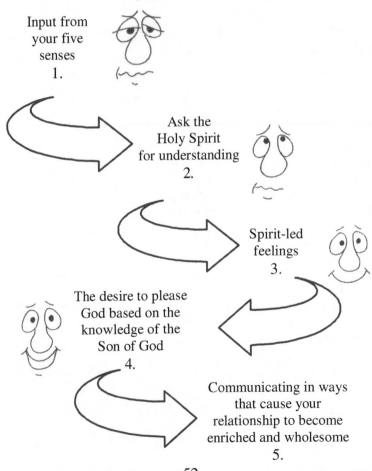

Input from your five senses
1.

Ask the Holy Spirit for understanding
2.

Spirit-led feelings
3.

The desire to please God based on the knowledge of the Son of God
4.

Communicating in ways that cause your relationship to become enriched and wholesome
5.

1. YOU HEAR YOUR SPOUSE, AND AT THE SAME TIME, RECEIVE INPUT FROM YOUR OTHER SENSES. THE WORDS AND WHAT YOU SENSE IMPACT YOUR FEELINGS AND EMOTIONS.

2. AT THIS POINT, THE SEQUENCE BEGINS TO DIFFER FROM THE PREVIOUS ONE. YOU ASK THE HOLY SPIRIT FOR SPIRITUAL UNDERSTANDING.

3. YOUR SPIRITUAL UNDERSTANDING CAPTURES YOUR FEELINGS AND EMOTIONS.

4. YOU NOW ALLOW YOUR DESIRE TO PLEASE GOD TO GUIDE WHAT YOU SAY OR DO.

5. YOUR COMMUNICATION RESULTS IN MARRIAGE ENRICHMENT. YOU GROW TOGETHER IN CHRIST.

Take the initiative. Do your part immediately to bring peace and restoration by speaking the truth in love because you were listening after the Spirit. Communicating with grace is simply allowing the Spirit of God to be involved in your communications, both verbal and non-verbal. Doing so enriches a growing, God-pleasing relationship. It results in mutual submission and biblical cleaving.

SPEAKING THE TRUTH IN LOVE AND LISTENING AFTER THE SPIRIT IS ALWAYS YOUR CHOICE.

(1 Peter 3:11 The Living Bible Paraphrase) "Turn away from evil and do good. Try to live in peace even if you must run after it to catch and hold it."

COMMUNICATING WITH GRACE REQUIRES SENSITIVITY
AND SKILL IN BOTH SPEAKING AND LISTENING.

The messages you send may be verbal or non-verbal. Your expressions, gestures, the look in your eyes, the way you position your body and what you do with your hands all send messages to your marriage partner. Often, what you say has less meaning to your spouse than the non-verbal messages you send. For example, your hands can say as much as your mouth. Hands can threaten and accuse, or they can welcome and receive.

Conflict is universal. It came with the fall of Adam and Eve, and will be with us until the Lord comes again. A flash of anger in the eyes, a back that is turned away, a look of disgust... all send a message. A gentle touch, a friendly smile and an open pair of hands to welcome someone also send a sure message. Your marriage partner will believe as much from your expressions and the non-verbal messages you send as from what you say. God has given you the ability to control the non-verbal messages equally as well as the words you speak. You gain this ability by listening after the Spirit. Some of the most enriching words you can speak into your marriages are, *Can you help me to understand, so I can be a blessing and not a burden?* These words will return appreciation, thoughtfulness and love to you. They will initiate an experience of encouragement and a meaningful moment of biblical cleaving.

(Ephesians 4:29-30 NKJV) "Let no corrupt word proceed out of your mouth, but what is good for necessary edification, that it may impart grace to the hearers. {30} And do not grieve the Holy Spirit of God, by whom you were sealed for the day of redemption."

FORGIVENESS: ARE YOU WILLING? GOD WAS.

*(Ephesians 4:31-32 NKJV) "Let all bitterness, wrath, anger, clamor, and evil speaking be put away from you, with all malice. {32} And be kind to one another, tenderhearted, **forgiving one another, just as God in Christ forgave you.**"*

Forgiveness must be communicated. It is a decision we make to have the same attitude God had with us. We have the opportunity, and the obligation to look upon our marriage partners with compassion and grace. Forgiveness is not to be dependent on the other person's actions. We can only do this and communicate effectively, when the words we speak enable and empower our *"Growing Together."*

- ☑ Words of forgiveness are free of corruption. There is no evil in them, but they bless, edify and encourage the hearer.

- ☑ Forgiveness always agrees with God's Word. Speaking forgiveness into the situation means you have been directed by His Spirit. You will bring to your marriage partner, the grace and boundless love of God.

55

☑ Grace, love and forgiveness insure that your marriage relationship will be enriched and strengthened.

As we close this chapter, shut the door on old ways of communicating with each other. Let go of all the disappointments, failures and wrong feelings. Let forgiveness open the door to the future, to God's blessings and a life of joy and peace. Speak the truth in love and listen after the Spirit. It is, after all, about *"Growing Together"* in Christ.

Chapter 5

YOUR PRIVATE GARDENS: TWO
PLACES OF INTIMACY FROM GOD

In God's perfect design for marriage, He provided two gardens of intimacy. In both private gardens He is present. The first is the garden of shared intimate physical relations. This is a walled garden. It is designed to be hidden from the sight of others. It is intended to be completely private. It is to be enjoyed exclusively by husband and wife. It can be a place that aids and affirms your experience of *"Growing Together."*

The second garden is the garden of prayer. This is as intimate a garden as the first one. It is designed for times of shared intimacy in prayer to the Lord. In it, the couple draws closer to each other, as they draw closer to God. Prayer affirms and reinforces spiritual intimacy with God and with each other.

Both gardens work in concert to provide the marriage couple a shared opportunity to experience the hand and heart of God.

THE FIRST GARDEN: THE MARRIAGE BED

(Genesis 4:1 NKJV) "Now Adam knew Eve his wife, and she conceived and bore Cain, and said, "I have acquired a man from the LORD.""

THERE WAS DIVINE PRESENCE AND ASSISTANCE IN THE FIRST ACT OF MARITAL INTIMACY AND REPRODUCTION. IT WAS GOD'S DESIGN.

God's Word declares that intimate physical relations are part of marriage, and that each partner is the exclusive sexual territory of the other. There are no exceptions.

(Proverbs 5:15 NKJV) "Drink water from your own cistern, And running water from your own well."

(Proverbs 9:17-18 NKJV) "Stolen water is sweet, And bread eaten in secret is pleasant {18} But he does not know that the dead are there, That her guests are in the depths of hell."

Men, look carefully at what the Bible says about a husband's view of his wife.

(Song of Solomon 4:12 NKJV) **"A garden enclosed Is my sister, my spouse...."**

(Song of Songs 4:12 The Living Bible Paraphrase) **"My darling bride is like a private garden**, *a spring that no one else can have, a fountain of my own."*

(Song of Solomon 5:1a NKJV) "I have come to **my garden, my sister, my spouse;** *I have gathered my myrrh with my spice; I have eaten my honeycomb with my honey; I have drunk my wine with my milk..."*

The Scriptures, through these writings, identify your wife in three distinct ways.

- YOUR GARDEN
- YOUR SISTER
- YOUR SPOUSE

YOUR GARDEN

The Holy Spirit inspired the beautiful words above. King Solomon wrote them concerning a married couple's intimate physical relationship. Your wife has been given to you for that which is private, exclusive and protected by God's design and agreement. The walls of this agreement are the marriage covenant. There is only one gate. The husband and wife give each other the only two keys to unlock the gate and release the times of joyful passion and refreshing.

Some married people use sex as a reward or withhold it for punishment. How can we give each other the keys to our private gardens and then refuse our spouse entry into the garden as a punishment? God never intended us to change the lock or keys, as a means of punishing our spouse.

No lock will open easily, if it is rusted from being unused or exposed to the wrong elements. The locks on our private gardens need to yield easily. What could cause them to freeze up or become unyielding? Perhaps a person's upbringing, wrong information, fear, or experience influences how he or she looks at sex. Some have a sense of shame. Others feel that sex is something dirty, unlovely or to be endured without joy. God designed sex to be a beautiful, mutually submissive experience.

YOUR SISTER

Your wife is entitled to all the politeness, deference, care, honor and assistance you would give any woman, who is one of your sisters in Christ. In your particular garden, she is also your wife. How much greater should your watchfulness and care for her be? Be aware of the delicate nature of her feelings. Nurture her. Love her as Christ loves the church.

God sees your wife as a Proverbs 31 woman. His Word declares her worth is *"far above rubies."* He has designed her to be a creative and capable woman. From her, great things will come that glorify God and give testimony to the indwelling power of His Holy Spirit. Jesus is her greatest fan. He leads the cheers for her. Join in the cheers with Him.

YOUR SPOUSE

The Bible teaches that your wife is special in God's eyes. Proverbs 31 says, *"Strength and honor are her clothing... She opens her mouth with wisdom. And on her tongue is the law of kindness."* She is a precious gift from the Lord. She is one with you. Treat her in ways that show you understand her value and the close-knit connection God has established between the two of you. Do so, and you will find you are *"Growing Together"* in God's garden of intimacy. It will be a garden of mutual joy and blessing.

GOD'S DESIGN FOR YOUR PRIVATE GARDEN

God intends your private garden of marital intimacy to be undefiled and pure. If we look to the first model we have of such a garden, we can learn a great deal about our own intimate relationships.

(Genesis 2:15-18 NKJV) "Then the LORD God took the man and put him in the garden of Eden to tend and keep it. {16} And the LORD God commanded the man,

61

saying, "Of every tree of the garden you may freely eat;
{17} but of the tree of the knowledge of good and evil
you shall not eat, for in the day that you eat of it you
shall surely die." {18} And the LORD God said, "It is
not good that man should be alone; I will make him a
helper comparable to him."

Eden was to be Adam and Eve's private garden. It
contained a great variety of good tasting, wholesome
fruit, waiting to be plucked from its trees. All Adam
and Eve had to do was taste and see how good it was.
Look at its design.

☑ It was a sinless place of peace and security.

☑ It supplied Adam and Eve's needs.

☑ Adam and Eve had dominion over it.

(Genesis 3:2-7 NKJV) "And the woman said to the
serpent, "We may eat the fruit of the trees of the
garden; {3} but of the fruit of the tree which is in the
midst of the garden, God has said, 'You shall not eat it,
nor shall you touch it, lest you die.'" {4} Then the
serpent said to the woman, "You will not surely die. {5}
For God knows that in the day you eat of it your eyes
will be opened, and you will be like God, knowing good
and evil." {6} So when the woman saw that the tree was
good for food, that it was pleasant to the eyes, and a
tree desirable to make one wise, she took of its fruit and
ate. She also gave to her husband with her, and he ate.
{7} Then the eyes of both of them were opened, and

they knew that they were naked; and they sewed fig leaves together and made themselves coverings."

WHAT DOES THE KNOWLEDGE OF EVIL TRY TO FORCE UPON THE MARRIAGE BED?

Eating of the tree of the knowledge of good and evil spoiled Adam and Eve's pure and delightful garden. If you allow it, the knowledge of evil will also affect your private garden. It opens the door to the *"desires of your sinful nature"* (Galatians 5:19-21). Ungodly thoughts enter into the moment. These become seeds of destruction that grow, until they overcome all the good that is in the garden.

*(Galatians 5:19-21 NLT) "When you follow **the desires of your sinful nature**, your lives will produce these evil results: sexual immorality, impure thoughts, eagerness for lustful pleasure, {20} idolatry, participation in demonic activities, hostility, quarreling, jealousy, outbursts of anger, selfish ambition, divisions, the feeling that everyone is wrong except those in your own little group, {21} envy, drunkenness, wild parties, and other kinds of sin. Let me tell you again, as I have before, that anyone living that sort of life will not inherit the Kingdom of God."*

From Galatians 5:19-21 we see that the *"desires of your sinful nature"* can bring the following into your garden.

⮌ IMMORALITY	⮌ LUST
⮌ IMPURE THOUGHTS	⮌ ANGER
⮌ DEMONIC ACTIVITY	⮌ SELFISHNESS
⮌ HOSTILITY	⮌ DIVISIVENESS
⮌ QUARRELING	⮌ ENVY
⮌ JEALOUSY	⮌ ALL KINDS OF SIN

In addition to your sinful nature, old memories can hinder freedom in your garden and cause you to feel shame or worse. These old memories do not belong there. They will choke the seedlings of love and grace that God placed in your garden. Guard your garden. Cherish and watch over it. Weed out what does not belong there. Do so, on a regular basis.

HOW CAN YOU KEEP YOUR GARDEN PURE?

God intends your private garden of marital intimacy to be undefiled. If you choose to, you can keep your garden pure. Only the knowledge of good (revealed through the counsel and understanding of God and His Word) counteracts the knowledge of evil. You have the opportunity to choose what tree you will eat from each time you enter the garden.

(Galatians 5:22-25 The Living Bible Paraphrase) "But when the Holy Spirit controls our lives he will produce this kind of fruit in us: love, joy, peace, patience,

kindness, goodness, faithfulness, gentleness and self-control... Those who belong to Christ have nailed their natural evil desires to his cross and crucified them there. If we are living now by the Holy Spirit's power, let us follow the Holy Spirit's leading in every part of our lives."

PRACTICAL STEPS TO A WELL CARED-FOR PRIVATE GARDEN

1. Make it your habit to remind yourself that God is the third party of your covenant private garden experience.

2. Be sensitive to your spouse's emotional and physical condition.

3. Find ways to make your spouse feel special.

4. Give respect and affection at other times.

5. Bring patience with you into the marriage bed.

6. Give your tenderness freely.

7. Let your goal be to please your spouse.

8. Always be gentle, never harsh.

9. Give no place to pain or force.

10. Give complete deference and respect to your spouse's inhibitions.

11. Determine what you both enjoy and explore its boundaries. (It is worth repeating the previous step. Give complete deference and respect to your spouse's inhibitions.)

12. Do something to make the garden setting special.

13. Do what is necessary to make yourself inviting and attractive to your mate.

14. Be aware of little distractions and tensions.

    (Song of Solomon 2:15a NKJV) "Catch us the foxes, The little foxes that spoil the vines,"

15. Make it your habit to remind yourself that God is the third party of your covenant private garden experience. (Repeating this first step on the list is not a mistake. It bears repeating.)

By staying clear of the lusts of the flesh, whose seeds spring from the tree of the knowledge of good and evil, you will eventually find your way to your own tree of intimate life. Your intimate physical experiences as husband and wife will be joyful and satisfying.

PLAN AHEAD, BEFORE YOU ENTER THE MARRIAGE BED.
LET PHILIPPIANS 4:8 BE YOUR PLANNING GUIDE.

---

*(Philippians 4:8 NKJV) "Finally, brethren, whatever things are true, whatever things are noble, whatever things are just, whatever things are pure, whatever things are lovely, whatever things are of good report, if there is any virtue and if there is anything praiseworthy; **meditate on these things.**"*

To meditate is think carefully, fully and thoroughly about something; to plan ahead, understanding the value of what you are thinking about.

Plant your garden with trust, delight and commitment. You will harvest love, joy, peace, patience, kindness, goodness, faithfulness, gentleness and self-control.

There is no shame, guilt, or loss of face found in a pure and holy garden. Make your private garden such a place. Enjoy the wonders of intimacy that God has created. He will bless your marriage and honor you when you do.

THE SECOND GARDEN: THE ALTAR

There is absolutely nothing more vital to a Christian married couple than shared prayer. It re-creates the conditions in the Garden of Eden before the fall. When you pray as husband and wife, your most inward thoughts, needs, and weaknesses are exposed and presented to God (and each other). You are, in a very real sense, naked and unashamed before Him. You will have nothing to hide from God (or each other), and can present yourselves as little children to your Heavenly Father.

In today's busy, distracting world, it is often difficult for Christian husbands and wives to find the time, and in many cases, the desire to pray together. However, the most intimate thing a couple can do is pray with and for each other. Praying together has two vital effects. First, praying together about circumstances and problems helps to remove their power to affect your relationship adversely. It builds bridges over the gaps that would divide you. If there are problems with anything you face, praying together will allow you to hear from God and go forward unhindered. Second, praying together provides enriching nourishment for your marriage relationship. Sharing times of prayer opens the door to *"Growing Together."*

Choosing not to pray together is a walk out of the garden of the altar, away from so many good things in life. When you fail to pray as husband and wife, you give the devil room to come between you. It stops God's life-giving grace from flowing into your relationship. God provides the garden of the altar so He can meet with you. He desires to help you discover the unbounding possibilities of your covenant marriage relationship. Come together to Him at the garden of the altar. He will bless you with every possibility to walk together to your destiny.

(Psalms 34:8 NKJV) "Oh, taste and see that the LORD is good; Blessed is the man who trusts in Him!"

God always welcomes you to his altar. He designed it to be a place where you can meet with Him, speak your desires, hopes, dreams and needs to Him, and appropriate His blessings. God's word tells us a man and his wife who trust in and call out to Him at the altar of prayer will be blessed. There, they can nourish their relationship with times of prayer, praise and worship in the Holy Spirit.

A SCRIPTURAL GUIDE TO A PRAYERFUL LIFE
TOGETHER AS HUSBAND AND WIFE

(Colossians 1:9-13 NKJV) "For this reason we also, since the day we heard it, do not cease to pray for you, and to ask that you may be filled with the knowledge of His will in all wisdom and spiritual understanding; {10} that you may walk worthy of the Lord, fully pleasing Him, being fruitful in every good work and increasing in the knowledge of God; {11} strengthened with all might, according to His glorious power, for all patience and longsuffering with joy; {12} giving thanks to the Father who has qualified us to be partakers of the inheritance of the saints in the light. {13} He has delivered us from the power of darkness and conveyed us into the kingdom of the Son of His love,"

The Apostle Paul's prayer can help you, as a married couple, to express the principles you have learned from these two garden teachings. I have provided an example below, of how you might personalize this prayer. Develop your own pattern. Establish prayer as a daily habit in your married life.

Husband: *"Father, we come to You, as one flesh, honoring You, and asking that the cause of Christ in our marriage be fulfilled. We ask, together as one in Your sight, Father, that You fill us with an ever-increasing knowledge of Your Dear Son's will. We want to be better able to please You and each other. We earnestly desire that You reveal Your wisdom to us, and that You place Your spiritual understanding in us. We desire to submit to each other, as we submit to You. Dear Lord, if we can share Your wisdom and understanding, we will build our marriage daily into a pleasing oneness, before You. It is our hearts' desire. We declare it as one flesh, and we commit ourselves to it, and to You."*

Wife: *"Father, we will try above all things, to live a life worthy of You. We always want to be pleasing to You. Help us to be fruitful in everything we lay our hands to as a Christian couple. Help us to increase daily in the knowledge of who You are and what You mean to our marriage. Help us to understand that the vows we took make You the most important and necessary partner in the threefold cord of our life-long commitment."*

Husband: *"We ask that You strengthen the bonds of our covenant relationship through Your power and with Your anointing. We acknowledge that we cannot do it ourselves. We need You, Heavenly Father, to help us enrich our lives together. Let us be willing vessels for the flow of Your grace. Help us love one another more each day. Give us patience and peaceful spirits with each other, and help us to rejoice in our oneness."*

Wife: *"We thank You Father, that You have given us the gift of salvation. Let Your principles, and nothing else, be the foundation upon which we build our marriage. Help us to see each other as gifts from You. Give us the ability always to speak the truth in love. Help us to live our lives in the context of Your loving inheritance. We thank You that You have provided us with a heavenly garden in the midst of a troubled world. We desire that it be a garden of peace and joy that we can share together with You."*

Husband and Wife together: *"Father, we thank You for delivering us from the power of evil and spiritual blindness. We are blessed with a place in Your kingdom. Dear God, we desire to cleave to You, and Your ways above all else. So help us, Dear Lord, to do so. We love You and thank You for each other. We pray in Jesus' precious name. Amen."*

PART II

GOD'S LOVE AND YOUR HEARTS

Chapter 6

WHAT IS LOVE?

(1 John 4:16 NKJV) "And we have known and believed the love that God has for us. God is love, and he who abides in love abides in God, and God in him."

A clear, concise description of the way God views love comes from one of our church fathers, St. Augustine. When describing the love relationship within the divine Trinity, He wrote,

"...love involves a lover, a beloved, and a spirit of love between the lover and the loved. The Father might be likened to the lover; the Son to the loved one, and the Holy Spirit is the Spirit of love."[2]

St. Augustine's example of love between the three persons of the Trinity illustrates its unique, primary characteristic. Love, by God's example and His

---

[2] Augustine's writings quoted from "The Relational Disciple," © 2010 Joel Comiskey. Published by CCS Publishing, Moreno Valley, CA, P. 38.

standards, is relational in its quality and function. In its simplest form, it is a connection between those sharing a common, unified resolve to give to each other, regardless of what it may personally cost them. Jesus certainly exemplified this in His willingness to express the will of the Father in giving His life for us. This kind of love is mutually shared, expressed and maintained, while being beneficial to all those involved. As with the example of Jesus, there is a spillover effect. God's kind of love in marriage goes beyond the borders of its covenant relationship to flow into the lives of others within its reach.

> *(1 John 4:7-11 ICB™) "Dear friends, we should love each other, because love comes from God. The person who loves has become God's child and knows God. {8} Whoever does not love does not know God, because God is love. {9} This is how God showed his love to us: He sent his only Son into the world to give us life through him. {10} True love is God's love for us, not our love for God. God sent his Son to be the way to take away our sins. {11} That is how much God loved us, dear friends! So we also must love each other."*

This book is about love, as God practices it and His Word defines it, in the context of sharing it with our spouses. In 1 John 4:7, the Apostle John tells us, *"...we should love each other."* In the original Greek language of this text, John's word for *"love"* is *"agape."* He writes that God is *"agape"* and that we are to *"agape"* one another. As we have illustrated, above, God's kind of love is both a reflection of the person of God and the actions of the Godhead. The word *"agape"* occurs at least one hundred and sixteen times in the New Testament. Jesus reaffirmed God's Royal Law of Love, which was first given to the children of Israel.

(Deuteronomy 6:4-5 NKJV) "Hear, O Israel: The LORD our God, the LORD is one! {5} You shall love the LORD your God with all your heart, with all your soul, and with all your strength."

New Testament Reaffirmation

(Mark 12:29-31 NKJV) "Jesus answered him, "The first of all the commandments is: 'Hear, O Israel, the LORD our God, the LORD is one. {30} And you shall love the LORD your God with all your heart, with all your soul, with all your mind, and with all your strength.' This is the first commandment. {31} And the second, like it, is this: 'You shall love your neighbor as yourself.' There is no other commandment greater than these.""

(See also, Luke 10:27 and Matthew 22:37.)

God considers His kind of love of the utmost importance. He does not view it as a suggestion. As the Scriptures above indicate, it is one of the most clearly communicated commands in the New Testament. It comes directly from Jesus. He means it to be a reflection of His heart at work in ours. As we grow together in marriage, we ought to increasingly display this love to each other.

God built us to thrive on His kind of love. It is part of how He originally designed us. At times, however, we fail to understand its value. There are those of us who simply do not know how to love, or be loved. Some of us are just not equipped for it. We use the word "love" in many ways, with many implied meanings. We say, *"I love you,"* or *"I love pizza,"* or *"I love to swim,"* or *"I love reading."* Those may all be true statements, but they do not pertain to God's kind of *"agape"* love.

In some marriages, love is elusive. It may have been lost, or never was there. One or both marriage partners may search for it, but cannot find it. Others think their marriage is secure in it, only to see it slip from their grasp, removing that one thing that made their lives together complete. Now they find themselves lacking in that one thing that should have defined their marriage, God's kind of love.

On the following pages are three counterfeit examples of what we commonly refer to as love. They characterize many marriage relationships. They will inevitably fail to satisfy, because they are not God's kind of love.

FIRST COUNTERFEIT: LOVE IS A SERIES OF UNCONTROLLABLE FEELINGS.

Love for some people, can be a series of intense, uncontrollable feelings, such as infatuation, lust or an unhealthy need to be wanted. For them, love becomes an emotional search for something that never satisfies and always seems to be out of reach. Their search for love becomes an abuse of the genuine meaning of *"agape."* It is a counterfeit of the real thing. It can only lead to disappointment and emotional damage. It will invade the marriage covenant like a cancer and destroy any hope of *"Growing Together."* Couples who think they have found love, because it delivers this series of feelings and experiences can be misled and confused about what God intended for them. For these people, life is out of control. They watch themselves being moved, without having any expectation there is anything they can do about it.

The consequences are inevitable, whatever they may be, including divorce. The feelings for each other were genuine, but could not be shared together, expressed fruitfully or maintained for life. They failed to meet the requirements of God's kind of love. Ultimately, love that is a series of uncontrollable feelings can lead to a lot of pain, disappointment, shame or guilt. Uncontrollable feelings are not part of God's design for marriage. He wants to fill your covenant marriage relationship with the wonders of *"agape"* love and all that goes with it.

SECOND COUNTERFEIT: LOVE IS A SERIES OF INTENSE CONTROLLING FEELINGS.

There are those marriages in which one or both partners find themselves being controlled by their spouse's feelings, such as jealousy, envy or a need to dominate and control. As with our first example, the direction of their lives is no longer in their hands. They feel forced into the journey. Life for them, as with those we have described in our first counterfeit, is like being in a boat in a fast moving river, without oars, motor or anchor. Someone or something else has the rudder. It seemed right to begin with, but now its direction and speed are wrong. There appears to be no way to get it to where it would be a blessing. Its momentum appears impossible to stop, and the damage is in the process of being done. This too, is not God's kind of love.

THIRD COUNTERFEIT: LOVE IS BOTH UNCONTROLLABLE AND CONTROLLING FEELINGS.

(WORKING AT THE SAME TIME TO DESTROY WHAT GOD HAS PUT TOGETHER)

In this third category, we find marriage partners entangled in what they sincerely thought was love. Now, they find themselves in the unfortunate position where their feelings are both uncontrollable and controlling. These feelings have one or both spouses trapped in the misfortune of experiencing the worst of our two previous examples, combined. The marriage is tangled in feelings and experiences that rob it of peace and impose a sense of helplessness and emotional damage. The couple become like puppets on a string, trapped in a relationship that is out of control. Obviously, this is not God's kind of love either.

THE REMEDY

These three counterfeit experiences of what the world calls love can be remedied by applying the simple, truthful definition of love, previously given.

> "In its simplest form, it is a connection between those sharing a common, unified resolve to give to each other, regardless of what it may personally cost them."

You will find unity, peace, joy and strength for your marriage by giving *"agape"* (God's kind of love) to each other. *"Agape"* is the vehicle of God's grace. If you desire to enrich your marriage and fulfill your potential for *"Growing Together,"* depend on *"agape."* Here is the proper, accurate assessment of the remedy, straight from the Apostle Paul's hand and the Holy Spirit's heart.

"Love never fails..." (1 Corinthians 13:8a NKJV)

Consider this application of 1 Corinthians 13:8a.

*When God's kind of love defines your marriage,
it never fails.*

Chapter 7

TENDER MERCIES

*(Ephesians 4:31-32 NKJV) "Let all bitterness, wrath, anger, clamor, and evil speaking be put away from you, with all malice. {32} And be kind to one another, **tenderhearted**, forgiving one another, just as God in Christ forgave you."*

*(Colossians 3:12-14 NKJV) "Therefore, as the elect of God, holy and beloved, **put on tender mercies**, kindness, humility, meekness, longsuffering; {13} bearing with one another, and forgiving one another, if anyone has a complaint against another; even as Christ forgave you, so you also must do. {14} But above all these things put on love, which is the bond of perfection."*

The hearts of a husband and wife can be anything from extremely hard and darkened toward one another, to soft and pliable, shining with the tender mercies of God's kind of love. Marriage enrichment depends on their consistent ability to keep their hearts soft toward each other. Having tender hearts, from which you display tender mercies, vaccinates your marriage against the bitterness, wrath, anger, clamor, evil words and malice that Paul describes in Ephesians 4:31. It paves the way for tender mercies to come from within, as a means of grace and a show of God's kind of love. Mercies are not really mercies unless they are defined by tenderness of heart and its corresponding action. To be tender is to be pliable, soft, gentle, easy, unresisting, giving, resilient and warm. It is all about motivation and attitude. A major component of *"Growing Together"* is the display of tender mercies flowing out of tender, loving hearts.

Tender mercies are vital to an enriched, fulfilling marriage. They are powerful gifts husbands and wives give each other. Here are a number of ways tender mercies operate in the covenant marriage relationship. Remember, they are a gift from God, the third member of the marriage covenant.

1. YOUR TENDER MERCIES TAKE DELIBERATE, LOVING ACTION TO BLESS YOUR SPOUSE IN EVERY SITUATION.

A prime example of tender mercies is found in the responses of Boaz to Ruth, as she gleaned in his fields (The Book of Ruth).

(Ruth 2:5-9 NKJV) "Then Boaz said to his servant who was in charge of the reapers, "Whose young woman is this?" {6} So the servant who was in charge of the

*reapers answered and said, "It is the young Moabite woman who came back with Naomi from the country of Moab. {7} "And she said, 'Please let me glean and gather after the reapers among the sheaves.' So she came and has continued from morning until now, though she rested a little in the house." {8} Then Boaz said to Ruth, "You will listen, my daughter, will you not? Do not go to glean in another field, nor go from here, **but stay close by my young women. {9} Let your eyes be on the field which they reap, and go after them. Have I not commanded the young men not to touch you? And when you are thirsty, go to the vessels and drink from what the young men have drawn.""***

*(Ruth 2:15-16 NKJV) "And when she rose up to glean, Boaz commanded his young men, saying, **"Let her glean even among the sheaves, and do not reproach her. {16} Also let grain from the bundles fall purposely for her; leave it that she may glean, and do not rebuke her.""***

Boaz knew Ruth was in need of food. He also knew she was vulnerable in the fields. He did two things to bless her. First, he provided her with a place to reap. He even instructed his men to leave more on the ground than usual, so she could have the blessing of gathering all that she needed. She could even enjoy the water his men would provide when she became thirsty. Second, she could enjoy the protection of being around Boaz' men, who had been commanded not to touch her. They would provide protection from others who were working close by. Boaz did not know Ruth would become his wife, but he unselfishly released tender mercies toward her.

2. YOUR TENDER MERCIES CAN BE YOUR REFUSAL TO TAKE ADVANTAGE OF YOUR SPOUSE.

Tender mercies (the tenderness of your heart in action) are merciful responses that refuse to take advantage over your spouse, when you easily could. In our example of Boaz, we saw he enjoyed a position of great leadership in which he could easily have abused his power over Ruth. He had opportunities to do so, both in his fields, and on the night she came to him at the threshing floor (Ruth 2:5-9 and 3:7-15). On the threshing floor, Boaz knew Ruth was fully vulnerable to him. However, his only thoughts were to do what was right in the sight of the Lord. In that moment, his heart was soft toward her. His response was tender and gentle. He did what was best for her. It was a display of pure, tender mercies.

How tender is your heart in those times when you have an opportunity to take advantage of your spouse?

Boaz was rewarded greatly for his righteous, tender, merciful behavior. Ruth became his wife. They would become part of the scarlet thread of salvation, as ancestors of Mary, who found herself with child by the Holy Spirit. You too, will be rewarded for your tender behavior toward your spouse, as it enriches your marriage.

3. YOUR TENDER MERCIES SEE YOUR SPOUSE AS PRECIOUS AND BEYOND EARTHLY VALUE.

Your display of tender mercies can protect, cover and encourage your marriage partner through times of discouragement, discomfort or stress.

Consider the tenderness that Joseph showed Mary when he found she was with child by the Holy Spirit. He disregarded his own reputation and comfort to protect and care for her. Joseph's example teaches us that tenderness of heart is sacrificial and protective of our spouses. He tenderly cared for Mary without regard to what anybody might have said. He knew what a precious gift she was to him and treated her accordingly. He freely gave tender mercies.

4. YOUR TENDER MERCIES REMAIN GENTLE AND UNCHANGING, EVEN WHEN YOU ARE CRITICIZED OR ATTACKED.

In every marriage there are conflicts. We have moments of misunderstanding and times we say things that hurt one another. In these instances, tenderness reacts as if it was a big cushion or sponge. It absorbs the attack in love. It does not retaliate. When the conflict has subsided, because of your tender response, there are new breakthroughs in *"Growing Together."*

5. YOUR TENDER MERCIES ARE COVERING AND QUIETING ACTS.

Your tender mercies should always watch out for ways to shield or cover your spouse from ridicule, embarrassment or shame. Whenever possible, let your attitudes and actions protect your marriage partner from these things. Stand strongly against turmoil, fear or confusion. As you do, embrace your spouse with God's kind of reassuring love.

I love Jesus' words in Mark 4:39, when He spoke to the storm. I have used them countless times when a calming word was needed.

(Mark 4:39 NKJV) "Then He arose and rebuked the wind, and said to the sea, "Peace, be still!" And the wind ceased and there was a great calm."

It is your covenant marriage responsibility to intervene in the midst of your spouse's storms, trials, disappointments and tragedies. Tenderness can be your gift, freely given without expectation or need of return. You can tenderly and quietly still the storms, as an act of God's kind of love.

You should always be aware of opportunities to exercise tenderness toward your spouse. It is an unselfish act that points to the loving goodness of God and the tender mercies He has shown us.

Your tender mercies are a deliberate act on your part. They are not simply reactive. They are proactive. Tender mercies are the ultimate expression of Christ as our Good Shepherd. They reflect His example. He tenderly cares for His sheep. He guards them with His life. He is a barrier to all that would hurt them. Your ultimate call as a Christian husband or wife is to be the expression of Christ toward your covenant marriage partner.

(John 13:34 NKJV) "A new commandment I give to you, that you love one another..."

(John 10:11 NKJV) "I am the good shepherd. The good shepherd gives His life for the sheep."

Chapter 8

TRUSTING HEARTS

Trusting one another is vital to every marriage. Trust, like so many of the issues already presented, rests in the hearts of both husband and wife. It is the glue that holds them in agreement and keeps them comfortable and confident in their oneness. Therefore, mutual trust must operate unchallenged in their hearts. When trust is compromised, it rocks the foundations of the relationship. If one spouse loses trust in the other, things destabilize. The marriage, as a covenant institution of blessing, will falter. Without trust, the wholeness of the marriage begins to come apart. It wobbles and staggers in weakness, and wavers toward the edge of failure.

TRUSTING HEARTS FEED ON FAITH IN GOD

Consider the diagram on the following page. It symbolizes the strength of the marriage covenant through the triangle formed between God, husband and wife. A triangle is one of the strongest shapes in

91

creation. In marriage, God occupies the apex of the covenant relationship triangle. Without Him, the covenant is no longer a triangle. It becomes vulnerable in its weakness. Every aspect of this covenant relationship triangle depends on His influence and participation. You get your strength to trust in each other from faith in God.

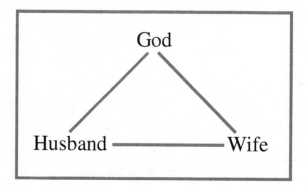

Trust between husband and wife gathers strength and staying power when both spouses allow their faith to draw them closer to God. As they move closer to God, they move closer to each other.

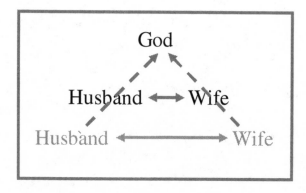

Trust is a heart issue. Encourage yourselves to nurture hearts of faith in God by feeding on His faithfulness. You will nurture faith and trust in each other.

> *(Proverbs 3:5-6 NKJV) "Trust in the LORD with all your heart, And lean not on your own understanding; {6} In all your ways acknowledge Him, And He shall direct your paths."*

> *(Psalms 37:3 NKJV) "Trust in the LORD, and do good; Dwell in the land, and feed on His faithfulness."*

TRUSTING HEARTS DISCERN THE BEST IN THE MIDST OF WHAT APPEARS TO BE THE WORST.

> *(Philippians 1:9 NKJV) "And this I pray, that your love may abound still more and more in knowledge and all **discernment**,"*

> *(Philippians 1:9-10a ICB™) "This is my prayer for you: that your love will grow more and more; that you will have knowledge and **understanding** with your love; {10} that you will see the difference between good and bad and choose the good..."*

The International Children's Bible (ICB™) paints an easily understood picture of the Philippians' love, growing because it has the ability to see through the lens of *"discernment."* The ICB™ translates this term as, *"understanding."* We can apply discernment (spiritual understanding) to husband and wife in the marriage covenant. Discernment provides you with the ability to see the truth when things appear, according to your natural thinking, to be otherwise. Trusting hearts can discern the best in the midst of what appears to be the worst. This kind of trust calls for a decision to have faith and hope in each other.

We learned in Chapter 3 that hope is one of the Seven Pillars of Love. Let's review the portion of Psalm 43:5 that was quoted under this sixth pillar.

> *(Psalms 43:5b NKJV) "...And why are you disquieted within me? Hope in God; For I shall yet praise Him, The help of my countenance and my God."*

Hope in each other goes hand in hand with hope in God. *"Growing Together"* requires that you believe the best in each other and expect it to come to pass. In 1 Corinthians 13:7, the Apostle Paul wrote, *"Love... hopes all things, endures all things."* Hope endures through all things (good or bad).

Hope goes beyond what might or should have happened. It does not dwell on what might not or should not have happened. It rejects the blame game. Instead, it discerns the possibilities for *"Growing Together"* past the moment. People with trusting hearts see the potential God sees. They embrace their spouses with forgiveness, hope and love. Trusting hearts give no place to the devil, and every place to Christ.

TRUSTING HEARTS PUT MEMORIES TO REST AND MOVE AHEAD TO GOD'S BEST.

Has the past created emotional boundaries through which trust in each other has not yet broken through? Would you be willing release these boundaries to the Lord, and trust Him to heal the emotional wounds that created them?

*(Isaiah 43:18-19 NKJV) "Do not remember the former things, Nor consider the things of old. {19} Behold, I will do a **new thing**, Now it shall spring forth; Shall you not know it? I will even make a road in the wilderness And rivers in the desert."*

God wants to do a *"new thing"* in your lives. He will do this *"new thing"* if you avoid the temptation to keep looking back at what was, or might have been. He desires to take your relationship to where you will find fresh, enriching times and seasons together. Make room in your hearts. You will grow to a new level of trust in each other, and move into God's *"new thing."* You will experience the joy of enriching your covenant marriage relationship, while *"Growing Together."* So, fill your life's journey with trusting hearts toward one another, and toward God. Walk into the future with a confident expectation for God's best. Along the way, you will experience the richness of the covenant marriage relationship He has given you.

TRUSTING HEARTS ARE TRUSTWORTHY HEARTS.

A TRUSTWORTHY HUSBAND
(There is no higher example than the Lord.)

*(Jeremiah 31:31-32 NKJV) "Behold, the days are coming, says the LORD, when I will make a new covenant with the house of Israel and with the house of Judah; {32} not according to the covenant that I made with their fathers in the day that I took them by the hand to lead them out of the land of Egypt, My covenant which they broke, **though I was a husband to them, says the LORD.**"*

God, speaking through His prophet Jeremiah, describes His actions toward the house of Israel as those of a *"husband."* He places this imagery of a husband upon Himself in the context of covenant. Through Jeremiah, God sorrows over the fact that the Israelites broke their covenant with Him, even though he was *"a husband to them."* We can ask, what made Him their husband. A study of the Scriptures leads us to the following conclusions.

1. God was faithful to His promises.
2. He cared deeply for His covenant partners, Israel.
3. He continually went beyond His anger and extended His heart in forgiveness.
4. He refused to abandon them.

5. He listened and made a way for them, even when it seemed they did not deserve it.

6. His heart suffered at times over their actions, but there remained a soft, pliable place for them.

7. He maintained a trusting heart toward those who honored their covenant relationships with Him.

8. He was, and is our example of a Proverbs 31 husband. He is *"known in the gates,"* (known publicly for his reputation) as honorable and completely trustworthy.

Husbands, the Lord is your example. You cannot be perfect, as He is. However, you can strive to honor your wife by being uncompromising and completely trustworthy. This brings great security and comfort to her.

A TRUSTWORTHY WIFE
(Our example - the Proverbs 31 woman)

*(Proverbs 31:10-12 NKJV) "Who can find a **virtuous wife**? For her worth is far above rubies. {11} **The heart of her husband safely trusts her;** So he will have no lack of gain. {12} She does him good and not evil All the days of her life."*

The Proverb tells us, *"the heart of her husband safely trusts her."* He bases his trust on his first-hand knowledge of her character. She is a *"virtuous wife."*

To be virtuous is to be morally upright, honest and honorable. The Hebrew word used for *"virtuous"* is *"chayil."* It has significant meanings in the context of this proverb. It translates as, *"virtuous,"* but also means *"strength"* and *"substance."* There is no weakness and nothing shallow in this trustworthy wife. She is completely dependable. Her husband's heart carries a deep, abiding trust in her. Her strength contributes to his.

When hearts are equally open and trusting toward each other, there is no room for mistrust. Both husband and wife see each other as trustworthy. They are affirmed in their relationship and able to continue *"Growing Together"* in their threefold covenant with God.

Chapter 9

FOR THE GLORY OF GOD

The previous eight chapters have painted a marvelous picture of God's amazing plan for enriching your marriage. Look again at the subjects we have covered.

1 GOD'S VIEW OF MARRIAGE
2 HUSBAND AND WIFE: DIFFERENT BY GOD'S DELIBERATE DESIGN
3 MARITAL LOVE: GOD'S DWELLING PLACE FOR YOU
4 COMMUNICATION: SPEAKING THE TRUTH IN LOVE
5 THE PRIVATE GARDEN: TWO PLACES OF INTIMACY FROM GOD
6 WHAT IS LOVE?
7 TENDER MERCIES
8 TRUSTING HEARTS

These chapters provide a clear set of instructions for how to take the *"Growing Together"* marriage journey. They direct us down the path of God's deliberate design for Christian marriage. This journey is characterized by truth-filled words spoken in love.

It has special times of private intimacy. It is to be enriched with God's kind of love, revealed in your tenderness and mercy. Finally, the covenant marriage is a union of two, who are one in God's eyes, trusting and being trusted.

WHAT REMAINS?

What remains to complete the picture? The answer is you, as husband and wife. Together, you provide the picture with meaning and purpose. It is your actions that will enrich the marriage covenant, and glorify its most vital member, the Lord God Almighty.

The book has offered you ways to understand and secure your relationship. Your marriage gathers its strengths from your agreement and oneness, as you journey to your destiny together. You are joined with each other, going somewhere. The proper mix of the characteristics found above will bond you together with great strength and testimony, to the glory of God.

A FINAL NOTE

When you practice these principles as husband and wife, God will bless your future and enrich your marriage greatly. Always remember,

- ☑ Your relationship is a God idea.
- ☑ You are joined in a holy covenant with God. Live your lives before Him in the knowledge that He is always with you.

☑ Marriage is a partnership of grace.

☑ God made husband and wife different by deliberate design.

☑ Honor Christ by submitting to each other.

☑ God has given you Seven Pillars of Love upon which to build your marriage.

☑ Speaking the Truth in Love is a key to your closeness and success.

☑ Listening after the Spirit pleases God and enriches your marriage.

☑ Forgiveness shuts the door on the devil and keeps the damage from your doorstep.

☑ Physical intimacy in marriage is a God idea.

☑ You will be blessed with two private gardens in your marriage, the marriage bed and the prayer garden. Tend them with care and value them with honor.

☑ Prayer is the most intimate and powerful thing you can do together.

☑ God's kind of love never fails.

☑ Tender mercies are a vital part of *"Growing Together."*

☑ View your marriage as an instrument to reveal the glory of God to all it touches.

☑ Walk a righteous path together. You will be blessed as God honors and enriches your lives.

Thank you for opening your hearts and hearing what is on mine. More importantly, thank you for hearing the heart of God for your lives. My wife Nancy and I pray for you, my readers, that God richly blesses your marriage, as His loving face shines down upon you together and gives you peace. Finally, that your commitment to covenant will glorify the Lord and send a message of how great it is to be *"Growing Together"* in marriage.

With every blessing, "Growing Together" in Christ,
Dr. Bob and Nancy Abramson

Appendix

SCRIPTURE REFERENCE TABLE

LEGEND OF SCRIPTURE REFERENCE TABLE ABBREVIATIONS

NIV   New International Bible

TLBP   The Living Bible Paraphrase

ICB™   The International Children's Bible

NLT   New Living Translation

All other Scriptures are NKJV - New King James Version

Dr. Bob Abramson

Dr. Abramson has extensive experience in cross-cultural marriage issues. He and his wife Nancy have pastored multicultural, international churches in New York City and the Fiji Islands in the South Pacific. He also established or taught in Bible schools and ministry training centers in New Zealand, Fiji, Taiwan, Hong Kong, Malaysia, Europe and the United States.

Dr. Abramson has a Doctor of Ministry from Erskine Theological Seminary, with a concentration on supra-cultural marriage enrichment. He also earned a Masters in Religion from Liberty University; and a Bachelor of Arts in the Bible with a minor in Systematic Theology from Southeastern University.

Dr. Abramson and his wife Nancy live in Lake Worth, Florida. They have five grown children and five grandchildren.

If you wish to contact Dr. Abramson, please visit
www.mentoringministry.com

Dr. Abramson is also the author of
"Just a Little Bit More - The Heart of a Mentor"
(Accounts of Cross-Cultural Mentoring and the
Lessons they Hold)

Made in the USA
San Bernardino, CA
17 September 2018